The Illustrated Story of President

GEORGE ALBERT SMITH

Great Leaders of The Church
of Jesus Christ of Latter-day Saints

The Illustrated Story of President George Albert Smith
Great Leaders of The Church of Jesus Christ
of Latter-day Saints

Copyright © 1982 by
Eagle Systems International
P.O. Box 508
Provo, Utah 84603

ISBN: 0-938762-08-7
Library of Congress Catalog Card No.: 82-70684

First Printing June 1982

First Edition

Lithographed in U.S.A.
by
COMMUNITY PRESS, INC.

A Member of
The American Bookseller's Association
New York, New York

The Illustrated Story of President

GEORGE ALBERT SMITH

Great Leaders of The Church
of Jesus Christ of Latter-day Saints

AUTHOR
Joy N. Hulme

ILLUSTRATOR
B. Keith Christensen

DIRECTOR AND CORRELATOR
Lael J. Woodbury

ADVISORS AND EDITORS
Paul & Millie Cheesman
Mark Ray Davis
L. Norman Egan
Annette Hullinger
Beatrice W. Friel

PUBLISHER
Steven R. Shallenberger

A Biography Of
GEORGE ALBERT SMITH

George Albert Smith, eighth President of The Church of Jesus Christ of Latter-day Saints, was born in Salt Lake City, April 4, 1870. He was the fourth generation of an illustrious Church family and a descendant of eleven pioneers: his father, all four grandparents, and six great-grandparents. His great-grandfather, John Smith, was an early stake president and patriarch and was left in charge of the Saints in the Salt Lake Valley that dreadful year when the cricket plague threatened the crops.

His grandfather, George A. Smith, for whom he was named, was a great leader. He was the youngest apostle ever ordained in modern times (twenty-one), and he later served as a counselor to Brigham Young. Although he died when George Albert was only five, his teachings had a great influence on the young boy.

John Henry Smith, George's father, was also an apostle and a counselor to President Joseph F. Smith. With such exemplary ancestors, George grew up in a home where the highest principles of religion and morality were taught. There were eleven children born to the family: eight sons, then three daughters. Three sons died in infancy.

George Albert, as the eldest, had a great deal of responsibility since his father was away much of the time on Church assignments. He began working at age thirteen in the Z.C.M.I. overall factory, while his father was presiding over the European Mission. He was employed for a short while with a surveying crew for the Denver and Rio Grande Railroad, and while he was working on the line to Green River, Utah, his eyes were badly damaged by excessive heat and sun glare. After this he became a traveling salesman for the Z.C.M.I. Department Store and later in his life worked in the Utah branch of the federal office.

As a young man, Elder Smith served as an MIA missionary in southern Utah, and after his marriage to President Wilford Woodruff's granddaughter, Lucy Emily, he was sent almost immediately to the Southern States Mission in Tennessee. In a few months his bride was called to join him there, and they served together for nearly two years.

George Albert became an apostle in 1903, while his father was also serving in the quorum. They were the only father and son to be apostles at the same time. In this calling his responsibilities were primarily with the YMMIA, especially scouting, and he received the highest award in that program, the Silver Buffalo. He organized the Utah Pioneer Landmarks and Trails Committee as well. He served as European Mission President right after World War I, and in 1938 he toured the missions in the South Pacific.

He was sustained as President of the Church May 21, 1945, at the age of seventy-five. Two years later he was in charge of the big centennial celebration of the pioneer movement to Utah.

A kindly, dignified leader, he was dedicated to the service of others. An example of this dedication is shown by his reaction when his prized Indian blanket was stolen. He said sadly, "I wish that individual had come and asked for it. I would have given it to him gladly, rather than have him become a thief."

He died on his eighty-first birthday, April 4, 1951.

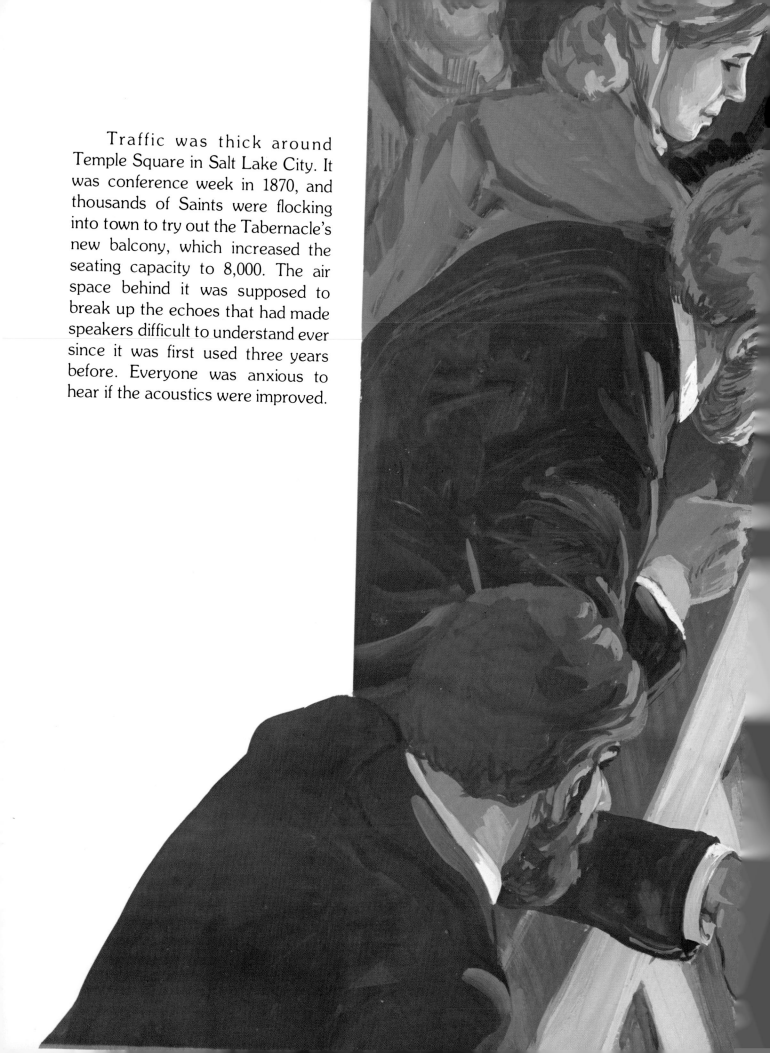

Traffic was thick around Temple Square in Salt Lake City. It was conference week in 1870, and thousands of Saints were flocking into town to try out the Tabernacle's new balcony, which increased the seating capacity to 8,000. The air space behind it was supposed to break up the echoes that had made speakers difficult to understand ever since it was first used three years before. Everyone was anxious to hear if the acoustics were improved.

Across the street to the west in a humble little home another important event was taking place. On Monday, April 4, a baby boy was born to John Henry and Sara Farr Smith. He was their second son, the first to survive. They had decided to name him George Albert after his grandfather, George A. Smith, who was at that time a counselor to President Brigham Young. His grandfather would sit in one of the seats of honor in the west end of the Tabernacle at conference.

"You look thoughtful, my dear," John may have said to his wife. "What's on your mind?"

"I was just wondering," she replied, "how they will keep the names straight?"

"Who? What names?" he asked with a puzzled look.

"The Church history books. All those Smiths. Joseph's family, and Hyrum's, and especially ours with two Johns and two Georges."

"You think we'll be that important?"

"Of course. It's your family's tradition. How will people keep from getting mixed up?"

"That's easy," John said. "All they have to do is start with my grandfather, John Smith, uncle of the Prophet Joseph, then alternate the Johns and Georges, adding the second name. Each is longer than the one before it, like this:

> John Smith
> George A. Smith
> John Henry Smith
> George Albert Smith

"That's a good way to remember the names," Sara agreed. And so the child was named George Albert.

George Albert had a happy childhood growing up in Salt Lake City. His first memories were of kneeling beside the trundle bed while his mother listened to his prayers. For him prayer became a way of life.

Next door lived George A. Smith, known as "Grandpa Nuts" because of the pine nuts he brought back from his visits to the Indians. He taught his young namesake that "there is a well-defined line between the Lord's territory and the devil's. If you will stay on the Lord's side, the adversary cannot come there to tempt you. But if you cross onto the devil's side, you are in his territory and you are in his power and he will work on you to get you just as far from that line as he possibly can."

When the stories around the fireplace turned to those of the early days of the Church, Grandpa Nuts could remember just what had happened.

"I was in the advance party with Orson Pratt and others," he would recall. "I saw this valley even before Brigham Young and helped plant the first crops right where this house is.

"The Saints had used up almost all the food they brought with them and we knew we'd starve if we didn't get something growing soon. The end of July is awfully late to plant, and we didn't know what would mature before the frost. We tried potatoes, corn, wheat, and garden vegetables.

"First we had to decide where to plant. The valley had many streams coming out of the mountains, and along these creeks the grass was green. But away from the water the ground sizzled, and big black crickets popped about like water on a hot stove top.

"We tried to plow a plot to plant and the first day we broke several plowshares in the sun-baked earth. Then someone suggested that we dam the stream and flood the ground to soften it. That worked fine and we plowed, planted, and irrigated our crops with water from the streams.

"More and more Saints came West. They all needed houses and food. Many small houses were built around the walls inside the forts."

"Why did they build forts, Grandpa?" George may have asked. "There wasn't a war, was there?"

"No, not yet. The Saints just wanted to feel safe from enemies, wild animals, and any other dangers they might not know about yet.

"The log houses were roofed with branches covered with grass and dirt. When it rained, they leaked. Covered wagon tops were hung over the beds and oilcloth over the tables to keep them dry.

"When frost came, the potatoes were only as big as marbles. Although they weren't large enough to eat, they were big enough to save for seed. Fall wheat was planted to grow in the spring, but spring was a long time away. The Saints grew hungrier and hungrier. They ate thistle roots, sego lily bulbs, wild rose berries, crows, hawks and wolf meat."

"Wolf meat? Yuk! How awful!"

"When you're starving, anything tastes better than nothing."

"I guess so," the boy concluded. "Are we nearly to the part about the seagulls?"

"Nearly," Grandpa would promise. Then he would remind the family that he returned to Winter Quarters to help other pioneers, so he wasn't in the Salt Lake Valley that next year.

"But my father, John Smith, the stake president, was left in charge," he explained, "and he told me all about it. As soon as spring came, he encouraged the Saints to plow, plant, weed, and water.

15

"They waited with hollow stomaches for the taste of fresh vegetables from their gardens. On the edges of the foothills the crickets were waiting too. The pioneers had forgotten about them until they began to nibble on the growing crops.

"They came crawling and leaping into the fields in black, crackling crowds, and they devoured the tender new shoots of the gardens and wheat fields. There was war now, Georgie, a battle for their lives. If the crickets ate the food, the Saints would starve.

"They fought those pests every way they knew. They beat them and burned them. They drove them into ditches and drowned them. Still they came like the devil's black legions, greedily gorging themselves on our precious crops.

"Your great-grandfather sent out the word, 'We must pray.' The message spread across the fields like the warm whisper of a south wind, so the war-weary Saints dropped to their knees and called on the Lord to save them."

"Then the seagulls came, huh?" the child would ask.

"Yes. They flew in from the Great Salt Lake in such great clouds they hid the sun."

"And everyone thought they were going to eat the best of the crops."

"I'm afraid they did," Grandpa agreed.

"But they gobbled up the crickets instead, didn't they?"

"Every last one of them. It was a miracle. The crops were saved and so were the lives of the Saints."

As a boy of five, George Albert had an experience with the Prophet Brigham Young that taught him a memorable lesson. John Henry Smith was serving as a missionary in Great Britain, and Sara wanted to take her family to visit her parents in Ogden. The children were anxious to see "Grandpa Apples" (Loren Farr) and hunt for some fruit in his orchard. But there was no money to pay to ride the train.

"We'll go to President Young about it," Sara announced. "He is president of the Utah Central Railroad and would probably be happy to get some passes for us."

She dressed young George in his black velvet suit and sent him the two blocks to the prophet's office with a letter asking for assistance.

Timidly the small boy pushed open the heavy wooden gate in the wall that surrounded the Church headquarters. Standing just inside was a large Scotsman.

"What do you want?" he demanded.

Shaking with fear, George Albert told him that he had come to see President Young.

"He has no time for the likes of ye," the man growled. But then the office door opened and a large man with a long beard walked out.

"What's wanted, John?" he asked.

"Here is a little fellow wants to see President Young," John replied and roared with laughter at what seemed a great joke.

"Show him in, John," the prophet instructed. The guard took George to the porch where Brigham Young stood. The president held the boy's hand, led him into his office, and lifted him onto his knee. Gently he asked. "What do you want of President Young?" This very important person, President of the Church and governor of the territory, treated this young boy with as much respect and kindness as if he were a famous man. George Albert had learned at that young age that great men always make time for those in need. When he grew up, he did the same.

Not long after this, George's grandfather died, and within two years, so did Brigham Young.

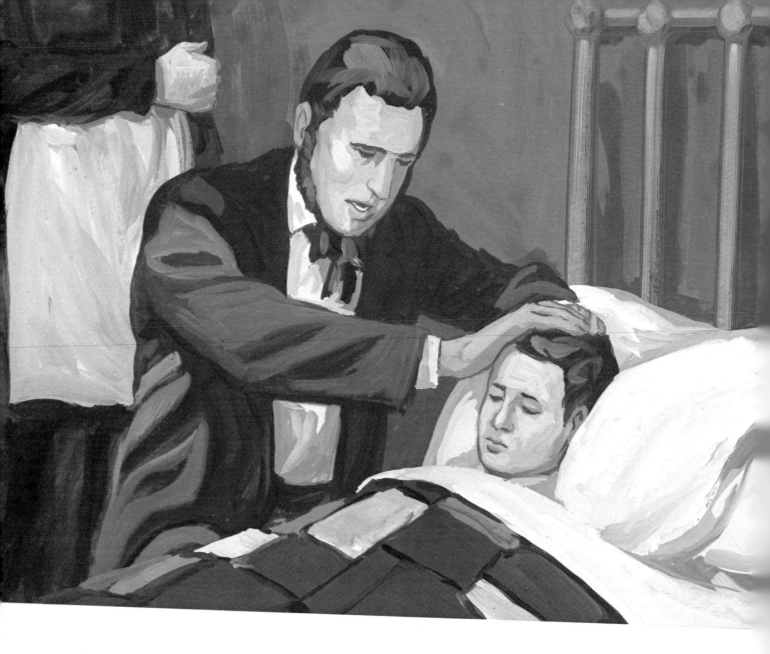

One day George Albert became very sick. He was as hot as fire when the doctor checked his symptoms.

"I'm afraid he has typhoid fever," he said.

The color drained from the face of Sara Smith. Typhoid was a word every mother dreaded to hear, and George had always been a delicate child.

"What can we do?" she whispered.

"Bed rest," the doctor advised, "for at least three weeks. Give him only liquids. Brew him some coffee."

George refused the coffee. He had been taught not to drink it.

"Bring me some water instead," he said, "and call our ward teacher. If he blesses me, I will be healed."

Brother Hawkes came quickly, laid his hands on the boy's head, and promised he would soon be well.

The next morning the fever was gone, and George felt much better.

"The Lord has healed me," he said quietly.

When George was eight years old, he was baptized in City Creek, a stream that ran between his house and Temple Square. When he was ten, his father was called to be an apostle and two years later was sent to Europe as mission president.

Living next to Temple Square put George Albert in the center of Salt Lake City activity. Just across the street he could watch the construction of the magnificent temple that was being built of syenite stone taken from Little Cottonwood Canyon about twenty miles away. He knew that the building was begun in 1853 and that stones had been hauled by horses and ox teams until 1873, when a railroad spur was completed to the quarry. As he grew, so did the temple. He would be twenty-three years old only two days before its dedication. In the meantime temple ordinances

were performed at the endowment house, an adobe building on the northwest corner of the square.

Within three blocks were the Social Hall, where balls, plays, parties, and priesthood meetings were held, and the Salt Lake Theatre, which was the center for culture and entertainment. Money to pay for tickets was scarce, but the box office accepted almost anything for admission: wheat, oats, pigs, animal skins, apple-sauce, sausages, hams, etc.

At the age of thirteen, young George went to Provo to live with relatives while he attended Brigham Young Academy. One day in class his teacher, Dr. Karl G. Maeser, said, "Not only will you be held accountable for the things you do, but you will be held responsible for the very thoughts you think."

This was hard for George to understand. It seemed to him that thoughts flew in and out of his head like birds on a wire. "How do you control them?" he wondered.

He pondered a long time. Suddenly one day an interpretation came to him. He wrote, "Why, of course, you will be held accountable for your thoughts because when your life is complete in mortality, it will be the sum of your thoughts. That one suggestion has been a great blessing to me all my life, and it has enabled me upon many occasions to avoid thinking improperly because I realize that I will be, when life's labor is complete, the product of my thoughts."

29

Shortly after he learned this lesson, George returned to Salt Lake City and found a job in the Z.C.M.I. overall factory. With his father away, his mother needed him to help support a growing family. A total of eight sons were born to John Henry and Sara Smith. Three of them died as babies. Finally, when George was sixteen, a baby sister brought delight into the hearts of family members and ribbons, ruffles, and frills into their closets. Later two more sisters were born.

During his youth George Albert held several jobs. When he was eighteen, he attended the University of Utah for a year. Then he worked for a short time with a Denver and Rio Grand Railroad surveying crew. While he was working on the line to Green River, Utah, excessive heat and sun glare damaged his eyesight quite badly. It was a permanent injury and made Brother Smith very sympathetic to the sightless.

In the spring of 1890 two young Z.C.M.I. salesmen, dressed in sporty clothes and traveling with a team and wagon, left Salt Lake City. James Poulton carried his flute and George Albert Smith brought his guitar. Playing, singing, and selling made a happy combination for this energetic and conscientious pair, and when they returned from the southern settlements in the fall, their books were filled with orders for goods from the local merchants.

The Lord had need for such zealous and congenial young men to encourage the youth of the Church to lead better lives and support the Mutual Improvement Association. George Albert was soon called on a short mission in Southern Utah to teach a better way of life.

The next spring he married his childhood sweetheart, Lucy Emily Woodruff, granddaughter of Wilford Woodruff, who was President of the Church at that time. One week later he left for a mission to the Southern States, with headquarters at Chatanooga, Tennessee. Feelings there were high against the Mormon missionaries. In fact some had been killed by mobocrats in that area. One night the mission president, J. Golden Kimball, and six missionaries were crowded into a very small and humble split-log lean-to of some local Saints in a wooded rural area.

About midnight they were awakened by loud shouting and foul language. In the moonlight they could see a group of angry people on the outside of the house.

President Kimball jumped up and started to dress, as the men pounded on the door, screamed threats, and ordered the missionaries to come out.

George Albert didn't move.

"Aren't you going to get up and get dressed?" President Kimball demanded.

"No," Elder Smith replied. "I'm going to stay in bed. I'm sure the Lord will take care of us."

In a moment the room was filled with shots. They seemed to be coming from all four corners. Wood splinters were flying in every direction. After a moment of calm, another volley was fired and more splinters flew.

"I felt absolutely no terror," George Albert later wrote. "I was very calm as I lay there, experiencing one of the most horrible events of my life, but I was sure that as long as I was preaching the word of God and following his teachings that the Lord would protect me and he did."

THINK ABOUT IT:

1. How is faith related to courage?
2. Give an example of this in the life of George Albert Smith.
3. Ask your parents about some examples in your own family.

After four months in the field, Elder Smith was transferred to the mission home to act as secretary, and his bride was called to serve the rest of his mission with him. By the time they came home, prejudice against the Saints had almost died out.

In 1898 George Albert was appointed by President McKinley to act as receiver for federal money in the land office. This source of income allowed him and Lucy to build a comfortable home on the lot his father gave him next to his own on West Temple.

"I wonder what all the excitement is about," George said to himself as he approached his home about 3:45 p.m. on Oct. 6, 1903. He could see that Lucy had visitors who were hugging and kissing her and talking a mile a minute.

He was coming from his work at the land office and planned to take the children to the state fair. When he passed the Tabernacle, the Tuesday afternoon session of general conference was still going on, but the building was so crowded he couldn't get in, so he crossed the street to his home.

Nellie Colbrook Taylor had seen him coming and met him at the door.

"Congratulations!" she exclaimed. "I'm so happy about it."

"Congratulations?" he asked. "For what?"

"You don't know?" Sister Taylor sounded puzzled.

"Don't know what?"

"Why you've been sustained to succeed Brigham Young, Jr., as a member of the Quorum of the Twelve Apostles!" explained the excited lady.

"That couldn't be right," George Albert replied. "There must be some mistake."

"I heard it myself," Nellie insisted.

"It must be some other Smith," he said. "No one has talked to me about it."

Sister Taylor began to wonder if her ears had played tricks on her and she'd made a dreadful error. She apologized and hurried back to the Tabernacle to get the story straight. Yes, George Albert Smith was indeed the new apostle. She rushed back to the Smith home to proclaim the truth and was followed by others anxious to offer congratulations.

George could no longer doubt that the message was correct, but he felt "completely dumbfounded and could hardly believe it possible."

It was true that his patriarchal blessing had promised "thou shalt become a mighty apostle in the church . . . ", but he had interpreted this to mean that someday, in the far distant future, he might succeed his father. But now? He was only thirty-three years old. He felt unworthy and unprepared. There had never been a father and son serve as apostles at the same time before. What if people were critical of this? He was bewildered and depressed. All doubts left him, however, when he was set apart and welcomed into the quorum. He was eager to serve with all his energy.

George Albert had always had rather delicate health, and in 1908 he suffered a serious illness that made it impossible for him to attend to his duties. With his family he went to St. George, Utah—the town named for his grandfather—to see if it would improve his condition. A special tent was arranged where one side could be raised so he might be exposed to the healing effects of fresh air and sunshine. He was so weak he could scarcely move. He writes:

"One day I lost consciousness of my surroundings and thought I had passed to the other side. I found myself standing with my back to a beautiful lake, facing a great forest of trees. . . .

"I began to explore and after I had walked for some time, I saw a man coming toward me. I became aware that he was a very large man, and I hurried my steps to reach him because I recognized him as my grandfather. In mortality he weighed over 300 pounds. . . .

"When Grandfather came within a few feet of me, he stopped. Then—and this I would like the boys and girls and young people never to forget—he looked at me very earnestly and said:

"'I would like to know what you have done with my name.'

"Everything I had ever done passed before me as though it were a flying picture on a screen—everything I had done. . . . I smiled and looked at my grandfather and said:

"'I have never done anything with your name of which you need be ashamed.'

"He stepped forward and took me in his arms, and as he did so, I became conscious again of my earthly surroundings. My pillow was wet with tears of gratitude that I could answer unashamed."

THINK ABOUT IT:

1. Why is it important to honor your name?
2. How did George Albert Smith learn this lesson?
3. What things can you do to honor your name?

After his recovery Elder Smith's life was full of civic and Church service. Right after the first World War he was mission president in Europe. He was also active in scouting for many years and received its highest award, the Silver Buffalo.

On May 21, 1945, he was sustained President of the Church. Four months later Word War II ended. He knew the people in Europe were destitute from the ravages of the conflict. He went to the President of the United States, Harry Truman, and asked what would be his attitude if the Latter-day Saints shipped food, clothing, and bedding to Europe.

"What do you want to ship it over there for?" President Truman asked. "Their money isn't any good."

"We don't want their money," President Smith said.

"You mean you're going to give it to them?"

"Of course we would give it to them. They are our brothers and sisters and are in distress. God has blessed us with a surplus and we will be glad to send it if we can have the cooperation of the government."

President Truman said, "We will be glad to help you in any way we can."

And so, from the Saints in America came load after load of supplies to the Saints in Europe. For the first time in history, Church members from all over the world drew together to feed and clothe their brothers and sisters. Tons of food and clothing went to non-members as well. The missions, closed by the war, opened again.

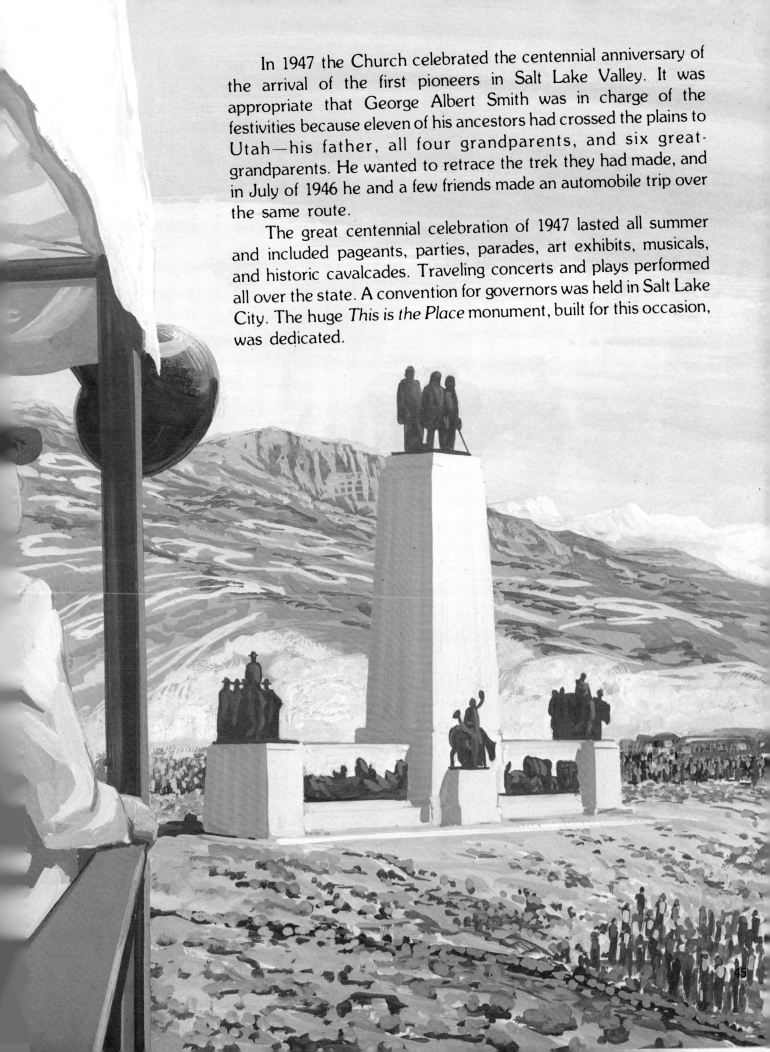

In 1947 the Church celebrated the centennial anniversary of the arrival of the first pioneers in Salt Lake Valley. It was appropriate that George Albert Smith was in charge of the festivities because eleven of his ancestors had crossed the plains to Utah—his father, all four grandparents, and six great-grandparents. He wanted to retrace the trek they had made, and in July of 1946 he and a few friends made an automobile trip over the same route.

The great centennial celebration of 1947 lasted all summer and included pageants, parties, parades, art exhibits, musicals, and historic cavalcades. Traveling concerts and plays performed all over the state. A convention for governors was held in Salt Lake City. The huge *This is the Place* monument, built for this occasion, was dedicated.

George Albert Smith was a dignified, slender man with hazel eyes, gray hair, a beard, glasses, and a kindly expression. He was the first Church president to appear in conference on television. He was responsible for acquiring and marking many Church historical sites, and he was one of the pioneers of aviation in the West. He was a special friend to the Indians, a champion of youth, and a great humanitarian. President Smith died on his eighty-first birthday, April 4, 1951. He had lived this creed:

1. I would be a friend to the friendless and find joy in ministering to the needs of the poor.
2. I would visit the sick and afflicted and inspire in them a desire for faith to be healed.
3. I would teach the truth to the understanding and blessing of all mankind.
4. I would seek out the erring one and try to win him back to a righteous and a happy life.
5. I would not seek to force people to live up to my ideals but rather love them into doing the thing that is right.
6. I would live with the masses and help to solve their problems that their earth life may be happy.
7. I would avoid the publicity of high positions and discourage the flattery of thoughtless friends.
8. I would not knowingly wound the feeling of any, not even one who may have wronged me, but would seek to do him good and make him my friend.
9. I would overcome the tendency to selfishness and jealousy and rejoice in the successes of all the children of my Heavenly Father.
10. I would not be an enemy to any living soul.

Knowing that the Redeemer of mankind has offered to the world the only plan that will fully develop us and make us really happy here and hereafter I feel it not only a duty but a blessed privilege to disseminate this truth. (*Improvement Era,* March 1932, p. 295.)

TESTIMONY

May the Lord add His blessings. I am thankful to be here today, and grateful for the way I've pretty near forgot I'm celebrating my birthday. Seventy-eight years ago today, right across the street, I was born. Now after all these years of traveling many parts of the world, associating with some of the great and good men and women of the world, I can stand here to say to you I know today better than I ever knew before, that God lives, that Jesus is the Christ, that Joseph Smith was a prophet of the living God, and that the Church that he organized under the direction of our Heavenly Father—the church that received divine authority—is still operating under the guidance of the same priesthood that was conferred by Peter, James, and John upon Joseph Smith and Oliver Cowdery.

I know that as I know that I live; and I leave that testimony with you and pray that our Heavenly Father will continue to guide us, and help us, and inspire us, and bless us, which He will if we are righteous.

May the Lord add His blessings, thankful for the comforts that we have today, and I pray that His peace and His love will abide with us forever and that we may be the means in His hands of bringing millions of his children to an understanding of his truths, that they too may be blessed as we have been blessed and are blessed this day.

This is my testimony to you—that this is the gospel of Jesus Christ—the power of God unto salvation to all those who will believe and obey it. And I bear that witness in the name of Jesus Christ, our Lord, Amen.